THE SECRET PLACE

OF THE MOST HIGH

How to Get There

"He that dwelleth in the secret place of the most high shall abide under the shadow of the Almighty."
Psalm 91:1

THE SECRET PLACE

OF THE MOST HIGH

Dr. S. Walker

Published by:
S. Walker Publications
P.O. Box 164048
Altamonte Springs, FL 32716
www.swalkerpublications.com

Printed in the United States of America

Scripture quotations are from the King James Version of the Holy Bible except where noted.

Cover Photo by: Sheila Walker

CONTENTS

DEDICATION

*This Devotional Study is Dedicated to
my two beautiful daughters,
Tanya and Candice*

Have you been struggling with an issue in your life that you feel should finally be settled? Especially because you've done everything you knew to do to bring a conclusion to the matter? What most of us misunderstand is that all of our own efforts, strength, ingenuity and strategies we design and put in place to solve our problems can be futile. Although God has given us the mental capacity and wisdom to solve some of our own problems, there is in all of us an inherent need for His help. Our strength, abilities and instinctive thinking equates to our mere humanness which may not be enough to bring us to the closure we're in need of. This is mainly where the underlying problem is concerning the persistence of some of the situations we're facing … we may have been trying on our own to fix things without earnestly seeking God's help.

Without God's help, we operate in and through a *natural* realm rather than a *spiritual* one. Even though we may speak of God as being the one who is helping us, in reality it's not His strength or ability at work … it's our own. This has us functioning in the flesh, which restricts God's divine and perfect will from being performed on our behalf.

Flesh in the Bible means more than our physical bodies. It also refers to the part of a person that thinks more earthly (*secular*) and less spiritually. It's a way of thinking that does not please God, in fact, it strives against Him. The Bible describes it as being "carnal minded."

Romans 8:7-8 "Because the carnal mind is enmity *(hostile to or towards God)* against God: for it is not subject *(does not obey or submit)* to the law of God, neither indeed can be. So then they that are in the flesh cannot please God."

"Carnal Thinking" conjures up bad thoughts and can have us feeling hopeless. As a result, we take matters into our own hands as if there is no God to help us.

Fleshly or carnal thinking is, without a doubt, a struggle for all of us at one time or another. It can be difficult at times to release the problems we're trying to solve and hand them over entirely to God. The reason for this is a lack of understanding about His character, which can strengthen our faith and give us peace during our trials.

How we handle the issues we go through in life, the challenges we face and the battles we fight, puts our faith on display. At times, especially during long and hard situations, this display may not be favorable in the eyes of others. But when we've turned them over to God, His power is seen at work in our lives. It is then that we are able to truly testify of our love for Him and faith in His ability to deliver us. In order to yield ourselves to God, we need a transformation of our minds and our thinking so that we depend on Him more.

Romans 12:2 "And be not conformed to this world: but be ye transformed by the renewing of your mind, that ye may prove what *is* that good, and acceptable, and perfect, will of God."

Trust in God is not the same as "Saving Faith." Saving Faith is the faith that we have in God's ultimate universal plan of Salvation through Jesus Christ. It is our acceptance of God's redemptive plan and living a committed Christian lifestyle.

Trust is the faith that has confidence in God's dependability and loyalty. It is having faith in His *faithfulness* which is another important part of living a more spiritual life.

Proverbs 3:5-8 "Trust in the LORD with all thine heart; and lean not unto thine own understanding *(perception, interpretation)*. In all thy ways acknowledge *(in Hebrew means to know, recognize "yada," submit)* him, and he shall direct thy paths *(direction)*. Be not wise in thine own eyes *(do not rely on self-sufficiency, your own strength)*: fear *("ra'ad" trembling; be in awe of or reverence)*, the LORD, and depart from evil. It shall be health to thy navel, and marrow to thy bones."

The Secret Place of The Most High ... How to Get There gives us a better understanding about God, His relationship with us as our Heavenly Father, how sufficient His Grace is towards us, the essentials of prayer and the power that is in the Word. The scriptural aids included will help us shift from the natural to the spiritual realm of thinking about our problems and how we respond to them. Knowing this, gives us the assurance we need of God's presence and guidance as we transition through the issues of life.

CHAPTER 1

LEARNING MORE ABOUT GOD

Proverbs 18:10 "The name of the LORD *is* a strong tower: the righteous runneth into it, and is safe."

Knowing the characteristics of God will help how we interact and become more intimate with Him.

GOD IS SPIRIT

John 4:24 "God *is* a Spirit: and they that worship him must worship *him* in spirit and in truth."

GOD IS INFINITE *(immeasurable)*

1ˢᵗ Kings 8:27 "But will God indeed dwell on the earth? behold, the heaven and heaven of heavens cannot contain thee; how much less this house that I have built?"

GOD IS OMNIPOTENT *(all-powerful)*

Genesis 18:14 "Is anything too hard for the LORD? At the time appointed I will return unto thee, according to the time of life, and Sarah shall have a son."

GOD IS OMNIPRESENT *(God is everywhere)*

Genesis 28:16 "Then Jacob awoke from his sleep and said, "Surely the LORD is in this place, and I did not know it."

GOD IS OMNISCIENT *(God knows everything)*

1ˢᵗ John 3:20 "For if our heart condemn us, God is greater than our heart, and knoweth all things."

GOD IS IMMUTABLE *(God is unchangeable)*

Malachi 3:6 "For I *am* the LORD, I change not; therefore ye sons of Jacob are not consumed."

GOD IS WISE

Proverbs 3:19 "The LORD by wisdom hath founded the earth; by understanding hath he established the heavens."

GOD IS SOVEREIGN

Daniel 4:35 "And all the inhabitants of the earth are reputed as nothing and he doeth according to his will in the army of heaven, and among the inhabitants of the earth: and none can stay his hand, or say unto him, What doest thou?"

GOD IS THE CREATOR

Genesis 1:1 "In the beginning God created the heaven and the earth."

GOD WILLS

Romans 9:19 "Thou wilt say then unto me, Why doth he yet find fault? For who hath resisted his will?"

GOD IS HOLY

Exodus 15:11 "Who *is* like unto thee, O LORD, among the gods? who *is* like thee, glorious in holiness, fearful *in* praises, doing wonders?"

GOD IS RIGHTEOUS *(Trustworthy, Read Numbers 28:19)*

Genesis 18:25 "That be far from thee to do after this manner, to slay the righteous with the wicked: and that the righteous should be as the wicked, that be far from thee: Shall not the Judge of all the earth do right?"

GOD IS FAITHFUL

Deuteronomy 4:31 "For the LORD thy God *is* a merciful God; he will not forsake thee, neither destroy thee, nor forget the covenant of thy fathers which he sware unto them."

GOD IS MERCIFUL *(God is sympathetic towards us)*

Psalm 103:8 "The LORD *is* merciful and gracious, slow to anger, and plenteous in mercy." *(Read Genesis 18:26, Psalm 25:6)*

GOD IS LOVE *(Love is His highest attribute)*

Ephesians 2:4-5 "But God, who is rich in mercy, for his great love wherewith he loved us, Even when we were dead in sins, hath quickened us together with Christ, (by grace ye are saved)."

GOD IS GOOD

Psalm 25:8 "Good and upright *is* the LORD: therefore will he teach sinners in the way."

NOTES:

CHAPTER 2

OUR RELATIONSHIP WITH GOD

Matthew 6:9 "Our Father which art in heaven,
Hallowed be thy name."

Jehovah/Yahweh *(from the verb "to be," which means "He is")* is one of the most important names of God in the Bible. Translated, it means "LORD" in our vision. It is the name God gave to Moses to describe Himself as being an eternal, infinite, immutable, selfexisting, consistent, trustworthy, faithful and all loving God.

Exodus 3:14 "And God said unto Moses, I AM THAT I AM: and he said, Thus shalt thou say unto the children of Israel, I AM hath sent me unto you."

Jehovah ... "I AM THAT I AM," in essence, this sacred and sovereign name expresses the powerful and intimate relationship God has with His people. To express this further, the name Jehovah is used in combination in the following ways:

JEHOVAH-ROPHEKA "God that heals"

Exodus 15:26 "And said, If thou wilt diligently hearken to the voice of the LORD thy God, and wilt do that which is right in his sight, and wilt give ear to his commandments, and keep all his statutes, I will put none of these diseases upon thee, which I have brought upon the Egyptians: for I *am* the LORD that healeth thee."

JEHOVAH-ROI "The LORD is my Shepherd"

Psalms 23:1 "A Psalm of David. The LORD *is* my shepherd; I shall not want."

JEHOVAH-JIREH "The LORD will Provide"

Genesis 22:14 "So Abraham called that place The LORD Will Provide. And to this day it is said, 'On the mountain of the LORD it will be provided.'" New International Version

JEHOVAH-NISSI "The LORD is my Banner"

Exodus 17:15 "Moses built an altar and named it The LORD is my Banner." New American Standard Bible

JEHOVAH-SHALOM "The LORD is Peace"

Judges 6:24 "So Gideon built an altar to the LORD there and called it The LORD Is Peace. To this day it stands in Ophrah of the Abiezrites." New International Version

JEHOVAH-SHAMMAH "The LORD is There"

Ezekiel 48:35 "The distance around the entire city will be 6 miles. And from that day the name of the city will be 'The LORD Is There.'" New Living Translation

JEHOVAH-TSIDKENU "The LORD is our Righteousness"

Jeremiah 23:6 "In his days Judah shall be saved, and Israel shall dwell safely: and this *is* his name whereby he shall be called, THE LORD OUR RIGHTEOUSNESS."

Jehovah also means God the Father who provides Redemption *(The God of Redemption).*

THE FATHER'S LOVE

The one important fact we should always remember, no matter what, is that God's love is given to us in abundance. So much so that He provided us with Salvation through Jesus Christ, which secures our relationship with Him. His love as a Father is unchangeable; it gives us protection and all of the benefits of being His child.

John 3:16 "For God so loved the world, that he gave his only begotten Son, that whosoever believeth in him should not perish, but have everlasting life."

Romans 5:8 "But God demonstrates his own love for us in this: While we were still sinners, Christ died for us." New International Version

John 1:12 "But as many as received Him, to them gave He power to become the sons of God, *even* to them that believe on his name."

1ˢᵗ John 3:1 "See what great love the Father has lavished on us, that we should be called children of God! And that is what we are! The reason the world does not know us is that it did not know him." New International Version

Ephesians 2:4 "But God, who is rich in mercy, for his great love wherewith he loved us."

THE BENEFITS OF BEING HIS CHILD

When we accepted Jesus Christ as our Lord and Savior, we became a spiritual child of God with special benefits.

Galatians 3:26 "For ye are all the children of God by faith in Christ Jesus."

John 1:12-13 "But as many as received him, to them gave he power to become the sons of God, *even* to them that believe on his name: Which were born, not of blood, nor of the will of the flesh, nor of the will of man, but of God."

THESE BENEFITS INCLUDE:

ANSWERS TO OUR PRAYERS
Isaiah 65:24 "And it shall come to pass, that before they call, I will answer; and while they are yet speaking, I will hear."

CHASTISEMENT
Deuteronomy 8:5 "Know then in your heart that as a man disciplines his son, so the LORD your God disciplines you."

DELIVERANCE
Psalm 91:15 "He will call on me, and I will answer him; I will be

with him in trouble, I will deliver him and honor him."

HEALING

Psalm 30:2 "O LORD my God, I cried unto thee, and thou hast healed me."

Psalm 147:3 "He healeth the broken in heart, and bindeth up their wounds."

PROTECTION

Isaiah 43:2 "When thou passest through the waters, I *will be* with thee; and through the rivers, they shall not overflow thee: when thou walkest through the fire, thou shalt not be burned; neither shall the flame kindle upon thee."

PEACE

Philippians 4:6-7 "Be anxious for nothing, but in everything by prayer and supplication with thanksgiving let your requests be made known to God. And the peace of God, which surpasses all comprehension, will guard your hearts and your minds in Christ Jesus."

GUIDANCE

Psalm 73:24 "Thou shalt guide me with thy counsel, and afterward receive me *to* glory." *(Read Psalm 32:8)*

Psalm 32:8 "I will instruct thee and teach thee in the way which thou shalt go: I will guide thee with mine eye."

OUR RELATIONSHIP

Relationships are noticeable to others based on interaction and representation. As a child of God and a benefactor of His love, goodness and grace, we are expected to:

SHOW OUR LOVE FOR HIM

Deuteronomy 6:5 "And thou shalt love the LORD thy God with all thine heart, and with all thy soul, and with all thy might *(intensity, passion, sincerity)*."

PRAISE HIM FOR ALL HE DOES

Psalm 103:3 "Bless the LORD, O my soul, And forget none of His benefits; Who pardons all your iniquities, Who heals all your diseases; Who redeems your life from the pit, Who crowns you with lovingkindness and compassion."

HONOR HIM

Isaiah 25:1 "O LORD, I will honor and praise your name, for you are my God. You do such wonderful things! You planned them long ago, and now you have accomplished them." New Living Translation

Psalm 40:5 "Many, LORD my God, are the wonders you have done, the things you planned for us. None can compare with you; were I to speak and tell of your deeds, they would be too many to declare."

BE OBEDIENT

John 10:27-28 "My sheep hear My voice, and I know them, and they follow Me; and I give eternal life to them, and they will never perish; and no one will snatch them out of My hand."

REMAIN LOYAL

Isaiah 26:4 "Trust ye in the LORD forever: for in the LORD JEHOVAH *is* everlasting strength."

BEHAVE AS ONE OF HIS

Matthew 5:16 "Let your light so shine before men, that they may see your good works, and glorify your Father which is in heaven."

NOTES:

CHAPTER 3

GOD'S GRACE
His Divine Grace is Sufficient for All of Our Needs

1st Corinthians 12:9 "And he said unto me,
'My grace is sufficient for thee:
for my strength is made perfect in weakness.'"

The Divine Grace of God seems elusive sometimes because it's not fully understood. There are many ways to explain what God's Grace really is and how it's received. However, the reality is, is that God's Grace is available to everyone. That's why it should be:

- sought after
- applied at all times
- appreciated with daily thanksgiving unto God

Divine Grace is God's provision of perpetual love for us. When we face difficult situations, we can sometimes feel separated from our Heavenly Father. We then feel as though there is a void in our lives which overshadows our faith. It is at these times that needing His presence can mean more than needing His help.

Understanding and accepting God's Divine Grace will provide us with the:

- assurance and confidence that we need to live a stronger Christian lifestyle
- confidence to annul the feeling of unworthiness
- source of power that we need to be happy and content

DIVINE GRACE IS:

FREELY GIVEN

Psalm 84:1 "For the LORD God is a sun and shield: the LORD will give grace and glory: no good thing will he withhold from them that walk uprightly."

SUFFICIENT FOR ALL OUR NEEDS

2nd Corinthians 12:9 "And he said unto me, My grace is sufficient for thee: for my strength is made perfect in weakness. Most gladly therefore will I rather glory in my infirmities, that the power of Christ may rest upon me."

PROMISED TO HUMBLE PEOPLE

1st Peter 5:5b "Yea, all of you be subject one to another, and be clothed with humility: for God resisteth the proud, and giveth grace to the humble."

DIVINE GRACE IS ABUNDANT WITH:

FORGIVENESS OF SINS

Ephesians 1:5-6 "Having predestinated us unto the adoption of children by Jesus Christ to himself, according to the good pleasure of his will, To the praise of the glory of his grace, wherein he hath made us accepted in the beloved."

KINDNESS TOWARDS US

Ephesians 2:7-8 "So that in the ages to come He might show the surpassing riches of His grace in kindness toward us in Christ Jesus. For by grace you have been saved through faith; and that not of yourselves, it is the gift of God."

PROVISIONS FOR ALL OUR NEEDS

Philippians 4:19 "But my God shall supply all your need according to his riches in glory by Christ Jesus."

When we become doubtful and make mistakes that displease God, we should ask Him for His grace and mercy. Given to us in abundance, our relationship with the Father will be restored. The Apostle Paul realized this personally and confirmed the power of God's grace towards us all.

1st Timothy 1:13-15 "Even though I was formerly a blasphemer and a persecutor and a violent aggressor. Yet I was shown mercy because I acted ignorantly in unbelief; and the grace of our Lord was more than abundant, with the faith and love which are found in Christ Jesus. It is a trustworthy statement, deserving full acceptance, that Christ Jesus came into the world to save sinners, among whom I am foremost of all." New American Standard Bible

NOTES:

CHAPTER 4

COMMUNICATING WITH GOD
Eight Essentials of Prayer

Psalm 34:18-19 "The LORD *is* nigh unto them
that are of a broken heart; and saveth such as be of a
contrite spirit. Many *are* the afflictions of the righteous:
but the LORD delivereth him out of them all."

THE EIGHT ESSENTIALS OF PRAYER

FIRST – SINCERITY

Prayer should never be an exercise to show how religious we are. Nor should it be a psychological activity that we perform to convince ourselves that we have the ability to change God's will for us. These would be considered hypocritical prayers. We should always pray that God's will be done in our lives.

James 4:3 "Ye ask, and receive not, because ye ask amiss *(wrong motives, inappropriately)*, that ye may consume *(utilize or use)* it upon your lusts *(your own pleasure)*."

Matthew 6:6-7 "But thou, when thou prayest, enter into thy closet, and when thou hast shut thy door, pray to thy Father which is in secret; and thy Father which seeth in secret shall reward thee openly. But when ye pray, use not vain repetitions, as the heathen do: for they think that they shall be heard for their much speaking."

1st John 5:14 "And this is the confidence that we have in him, that, if we ask any thing according to his will, he heareth us."

SECOND –ASSURANCE

God is able and wants to provide for us and help us with our problems. Worriedness shows a lack of faith and trust in His love for us. When we ask for His help, we should always thank and praise Him to show our trust and appreciation.

Philippians 4:6 "Don't worry about anything, but in everything, through prayer and petition with thanksgiving, let your requests be made known to God." Holman Christian Standard Bible

Matthew 6:25 and 27 "Therefore I tell you, do not worry about your life, what you will eat or drink; or about your body, what you will wear. Is not life more important than food, and the body more important than clothes? Who of you by worrying can add a single hour to his life?" New International Version

THIRD – LETTING GO

Releasing our hold on a situation and becoming humble is also required in prayer. We can't ask for God's help and still be in control. We have to turn the entire situation over to Him.

Proverbs 3:5-6 "Trust in the LORD with all thine heart; and lean not unto thine own understanding. In all thy ways acknowledge him, and he shall direct thy paths."

1st Peter 5:7 "Casting all your cares upon him; for He careth for you."

FOURTH - REVERENCE

Prayer is how we communicate with God. Therefore, we should view prayer as an exceptional experience that requires reverence and awe of Him as He welcomes us into His presence. Before we pray asking God for anything we should first acknowledge Him by talking about His goodness, His greatness and how much we appreciate Him.

Matthew 6:9-10 "After this manner therefore pray ye: Our Father which art in heaven, Hallowed be thy name. Thy kingdom come, Thy will be done in earth, as *it is* in heaven."

1st Chronicles 16:8 "Give thanks unto the LORD, call upon his name, make known his deeds among the people."

Psalm 95: 1-2 "O come, let us sing unto the LORD: let us make a joyful noise to the rock of our salvation. Let us come before his presence with thanksgiving, and make a joyful noise unto him with psalms."

FIFTH - CONFESSION

After acknowledging Him, we should talk about ourselves by confessing our sins, shortcomings, disobedience and the grief we feel because of it. This part of prayer is so personally convicting, that it has the tendency to be omitted. To not confess of our faults is, in and of itself, a sin because it suggests that we are equal to God.

Romans 3:23 "For all have sinned and come short of the Glory of God."

James 5:16 "Confess *your* faults one to another, and pray one for another, that ye may be healed. The effectual *(powerful, able)* fervent prayer *(passionate, truthful)* of a righteous *(honest, up-right)* man availeth much."

Psalm 139:23-24 "Search me, O God, and know my heart; test me and know my anxious thoughts. See if there is any offensive way in me, and lead me in the way everlasting." New International Version

*1ˢᵗ **John 1:9*** "If we confess our sins, he is faithful and just to forgive us *our* sins, and to cleanse us from all unrighteousness."

SIXTH – FORGIVENESS

Not being able to forgive is another hindrance to our prayers. When we refuse to forgive we stabilize a blockage between God and ourselves. If we have a problem with forgiving, we should ask for His help. Forgiveness plays a very important role in getting our prayers answered.

Matthew 18:21-22 "Then came Peter to him, and said, Lord, How oft shall my brother sin against me, and I forgive him? till seven times? Jesus saith unto him, I say not unto thee, Until seven times: but, Until seventy times seven."

Psalm 66:18 "If I regard iniquity in my heart, the Lord will not hear me."

SEVENTH – THE INDWELLING OF THE HOLY SPIRIT

When we accepted Jesus Christ in our hearts, so that He can be Lord over our lives, we received the indwelling of the Holy Spirit, who does the following:

a) Transforms our natural bodies into temples

1st Corinthians 3:16 "Do you know that you are God's temple and that God's Spirit dwells in you?" English Standard Version

b) Provides us with a Holy Baptism *(a new beginning)*

Acts 11:16 "Then I remembered what the Lord had said: 'John baptized with water, but you will be baptized with the Holy Spirit.'" International Standard Version

Matthew 3:11 "I baptize you with water for repentance. But after me will come one who is more powerful than I, whose sandals I am not fit to carry. He will baptize you with the Holy Spirit and with fire."

c) Gives us an awareness to know and to do the right thing without being taught

1st John 2:27 "But the anointing which ye have received of him abideth in you, and ye need not that any man teach you: but as the same anointing teacheth you of all things, and is truth, and is no lie, and even as it hath taught you, ye shall abide in him."

d) Makes us a receiver of spiritual power

Ezekiel 36:27 "And I will put my Spirit within you, and cause you to walk in my statutes, and you shall keep my judgments, and do them." American King James Version

When we commit our lives to Christ, The Holy Spirit begins to live within us. He is therefore, always present to help us with our prayers. At times when we can't find the words to express what's in our hearts, He says them for us by interceding on our behalf.

Romans 8:26-27 "Likewise the Spirit helps us in our weakness. For we do not know what to pray for as we ought, but the Spirit himself intercedes for us with groanings too deep for words. And he who searches hearts knows what is the mind of the Spirit, because the Spirit intercedes for the saints according to the will of God." English Standard Version

EIGHT – HOW TO END PRAYER

Jesus is the gateway to the Father because of His death, burial and resurrection. His position is now in Heaven where He is seated on the right hand of the Father making intercession for us. Therefore, we should end our prayers by saying "In the name of Jesus, Amen *(truly, or let it be)*."

John 14:6 "Jesus saith unto him, I am the way, the truth, and the life: no man cometh unto the Father, but by me."

Hebrews 10:12 "But this man *(Jesus),* after he had offered one sacrifice for sins forever, sat down on the right hand of God."

Hebrews 7:25 "Therefore he is able, once and forever, to save those who come to God through him. He lives forever to intercede with God on their behalf." New Living Translation

John 14:13 "And whatsoever ye shall ask in my name, that will I do, that the Father may be glorified in the Son."

NOTES:

CHAPTER 5

LEARNING MORE THROUGH GOD'S WORD
God's Word for Power

Hebrews 4:12 "For the word of God *is* quick, and
powerful, and sharper than any two-edged sword,
piercing even to the dividing asunder of soul and
spirit, and of the joints and marrow, and *is* a
discerner of the thoughts and intents of the heart."

HEARING THE WORD OF GOD

The Word of God comes to us through preaching and teaching. Although we may feel inspired by these messages, some of the deeper meaning of what is being said is not always heard or retained.

When the Word of God goes forth *(preached or taught)* it is intended to accomplish something in our lives. This changes those words into deeper prophetic words *(messages from God which may or may not include predictions)*, which is why we should be very attentive. This is extremely important so that we receive the encouragement, instructions and knowledge He wants us to have.

Isaiah 55:10-11 "For as the rain comes down, and the snow from heaven, and returns not thither, but waters the earth, and makes it bring forth and bud, that it may give seed to the sower, and bread to the eater: So shall my word be that goes forth out of my mouth: it shall not return to me void, but it shall accomplish that which I please, and it shall prosper in the thing whereto I sent it." American King James Edition

Think of it as God wanting to speak to you personally to help you get through your trying situation.

Numbers 9:8 "Moses answered, 'Wait here until I have received instructions for you from the LORD.'" New Living Translation

Psalm 85:8 "I will hear what God the LORD will speak: for he will speak peace unto his people, and to his saints: but let them not turn again to folly."

1ˢᵗ Samuel 9:27 "As they were going down at the end of the city, Samuel said to Saul, Bid the servant pass on before us *(and he passed on)*, but stand thou still first, that I may cause thee to hear the word of God." American Standard Version

RETENTION

The reason why change in our situation may be difficult, or why encouragement seems to last only briefly when we hear the Word of God is retention *(the ability to remember or recollect what we've heard)*. There are several reasons for a lack of retention which are linked together to produce a serious and offensive spiritual condition known as a "form of godliness."

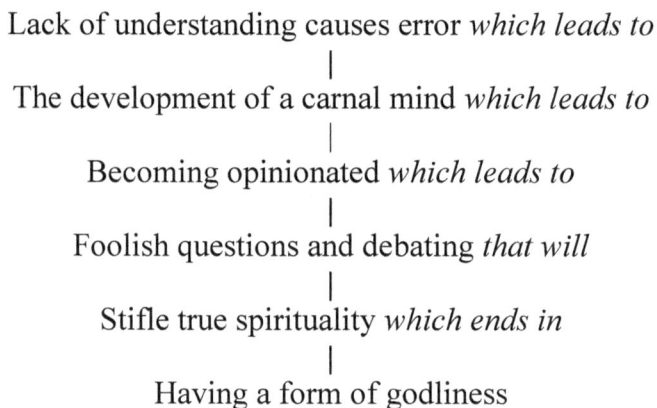

Lack of understanding causes error *which leads to*
|
The development of a carnal mind *which leads to*
|
Becoming opinionated *which leads to*
|
Foolish questions and debating *that will*
|
Stifle true spirituality *which ends in*
|
Having a form of godliness

2ⁿᵈ Timothy 3:7 "Ever learning, and never able to come to the knowledge of the truth."

A good example of this is when the Sadducees questioned Jesus about the resurrection.

Matthew 22:23-32 "The same day came to him the Sadducees, which say that there is no resurrection, and asked him, Saying, Master, Moses said, If a man die, having no children, his brother shall marry his wife, and raise up seed unto his brother. Now there were with us seven brethren: and the first, when he had married a wife, deceased, and, having no issue, left his wife unto his brother: Likewise the second also, and the third, unto the seventh. And last of all the woman died also. Therefore in the resurrection whose wife shall she be of the seven? For they all had her. Jesus answered and said unto them, Ye do err, not knowing the scriptures, nor the power of God. For in the resurrection they neither marry, nor are given in marriage, but are as the angels of God in heaven. But as touching the resurrection of the dead, have ye not read that which was spoken unto you by God, saying, I am the God of Abraham, and the God of Isaac, and the God of Jacob? God is not the God of the dead, but of the living."

In order to discipline ourselves to listen to God's spoken Word more carefully so that we retain it, we should understand that:

THE WORD OF GOD HELPS US TO BE PRODUCTIVE

God's Word is compared to seeds that are sown in different types of soil, all of which are not conducive to yielding a good harvest. Soil that is able to retain the seed until it produces an abundance of fruit is good soil. *(Read Matthew 8:5-8)*

Luke 8:8 "And others fell on good ground, and sprang up, and bore fruit an hundredfold *(a hundred times more)*. And when he had said these things, he cried, He that hath ears to hear, let him hear."

GOD'S WORD IS INFALLIBLE

The Word of God is absolute *(unquestionable)* which means it is trustworthy and the instructions that it gives to us is of great value; if we listen and take heed.

Matthew 5:18 "For verily I say unto you, Till heaven and earth pass, one jot or one tittle shall in no wise pass from the law, till all be fulfilled."

Psalm 119:152 "Long ago I learned from your statutes that you established them to last forever." New International Version

THE WORD OF GOD IS LIBERATING

When the truth of God's Word is received, it produces freedom.

John 8:31-32 "Then said Jesus to those Jews which believed on him, If ye continue in my word, then are ye my disciples indeed; And ye shall know the truth, and the truth shall make you free."

THE WORD OF GOD IS LIVING AND ACTIVE

Hebrews 4:12 "For the word of God is alive and powerful. It is sharper than the sharpest two-edged sword, cutting between soul and spirit, between joint and marrow. It exposes our innermost thoughts and desires." New Living Translation

GOD'S WORD GIVES US GUIDANCE

Without God's Word we'll lack control and cause others to criticize our spirituality. We need the guidance of God's Word to not only control us but to convict, strengthen, bless and empower us.

Exodus 32:25 "Now when Moses saw that the people were out of control--for Aaron had let them get out of control to be a derision among their enemies." New American Standard

IT'S THE WORD OF GOD, NOT FLATTERING WORDS OF MAN THAT PRODUCES GOOD WORKS IN US

2ⁿᵈ Timothy 4:3 "For the time will come when they will not en-dure sound doctrine; but after their own lusts shall they heap to themselves teachers, having itching ears."

1ˢᵗ Thessalonians 2:13 "And we also thank God constantly for this, that when you received the word of God, which you heard from us, you accepted it not as the word of men but as what it really is, the word of God, which is at work in you believers." English Standard Version

GOD'S WORD STRENGTHENS OUR FAITH

Romans 10:17 "So then, Faith cometh by hearing the Word of God."

GOD'S WORD LEADS US TO FULFILLMENT

Our destiny and purpose is realized more by hearing and doing what we learn in God's Word. This is how we gain the assurance, understanding and confidence we need to overcome our trials so that we move forward to achieve our goals.

Joshua 1:8 "This book of the law shall not depart out of thy mouth; but thou shalt meditate therein day and night, that thou mayest observe to do according to all that is written therein: for then thou shalt make thy way prosperous, and then thou shalt have good success."

DAILY BIBLE STUDY

Aside from hearing, we should read and study God's Word on a daily basis. To take away some of the apprehensive feelings that can come with trying to accomplish this goal, we should:

1. Schedule a specific time to read the Bible
2. Study a few verses before or after daily prayer
3. Read as much as we have time to study
4. Follow the study time-frame listed in our Bible
5. Go over the sermon we heard at church
6. Invest in a multi-translation Bible

NOTES:

CHAPTER 6

IT'S TIME TO MOVE

It's time to shift your thinking regarding the
situation you're facing or struggling with from
a natural perception to a spiritual one.

*Psalm 91:1 "He that dwelleth in the secret place
of the most High shall abide under the shadow
of the Almighty."*

It's time to change your perception, attitude, and confession *(which portrays your true thoughts about your problem and its resolve)*. You've stayed in your current mindset and way of thinking long enough. It's time to apply what you've learned and begin to think about your situation spiritually. Changing your mindset and putting God's Word into action will give you peace during your trial. This change should include seclusion so that you are alone with God, like a child with his father. It is in the spiritual environment that you will:

- settle your mind so that you feel safe
- find confidence
- gain insight into whatever it is that is troubling you
- see a more positive outcome

Psalm 91:1 "He that dwelleth in the secret place of the Most High shall abide under the shadow of the Almighty."

Interpreting this verse for personal application it means that the person who abides or settles into the secluded place of God has moved under His Divine overshadowing *(meaning the protection of God's omnipotent power)*.

It is here, in the "secret place" that spiritual instructions are given, where God encourages and empowers His people so that they are able to overcome their anxieties. Abiding under the shadow of The Almighty, the person will receive a new perception of themselves and see their problems in a different light. This is because while being in "the secret place of the Most High," they are able to shift from the natural realm into the spiritual realm. Being in this atmosphere will also strengthen their faith so that they can believe and trust God more for a positive and victorious outcome to their issues.

This happens because they've moved spiritually, mentally and physically, making a threefold transition necessary to dwell in "the secret place of the Most High." Again, the threefold transition is:

1. from the natural to a more spiritual way of thinking and responding *(releasing control of the problem to gain more faith and trust in God)*
2. mental *(a change and renewing of the mind)*
3. physical *(a change of environment)*

MAKING THE TRANSITION

Going to "the secret place of the Most High" means that you have decided to seek God regarding your problems. You want to know His plans for you and what actions you should take. You want to be in His presence to receive Divine wisdom, insight and instructions that will not only give you victory, but peace during your trial.

To help you move into "the secret place of the Most High" and become more spiritually minded, let's use moving from one location to another as an example.

The first thing you would do is decide on the place you are going to move. You've looked everywhere for help with your problems, but you were unsuccessful. Finally, you've found the perfect place ... "the secret place of the Most High."

The second thing you would do is pack your belongings; this would be your problems. Remember to pack every part of it, not just the part that is most pressing at the moment. Take the whole matter with you because beneath every set of issues are root causes *(cause and effect)*.

The third thing you would do is schedule a moving date. Don't forget that we're including a physical time of quiet and seclusion in the presence of God. We learn from reading the Bible that moving away from crowds and being alone to pray and seek God's help was a spiritual practice. Jesus, Moses, the Prophets, Paul, and many others moved into "the secret place of the Most High" to pray and inquire of God. Schedule your time to be alone with God so that you are not concerned about the cares of life for a little while. You want to spend this time focusing on your spirituality and help with your problems.

And finally, the fourth thing you would do is settle into your new residence. The same is true when you move into "the secret place of the Most High." You have to settle into this Holy environment, so don't expect a sudden change of your mindset and solution to your problems, this would be a temporary shift in your emotional state. It takes time to hear from God, which means that you have to plan to be in His presence for a while.

Through quiet prayer, become acquainted with God whose shadow you've moved under. Then acknowledge His presence by giving Him praise. After a while, begin to speak to Him about your situation without apprehension, shame, fear or doubt. Be confident that He is your present *(current, existing)* help. Know that He is there and that you don't have to look for Him. After all, you've moved into His place, the place where He dwells. Talk to Him with a trusting heart.

♦*You will eventually have to go back out into the natural realm and of course be faced with a whole new set of issues...that's just the reality of life. But you've increased your places of residency to have a personal retreat ... "the secret place of the Most High." When life presents its problems and situations that burden you down or have you searching for answers, move and spend time under the shadow of The Almighty.*

NOTES:

CHAPTER 7

POWER SCRIPTURES
While in the *Secret Place of the Most High*,
personalize and apply these Scriptures
to your situation.

Romans 10:17 "So then faith cometh by
hearing, and hearing by the word of God."

POWER SCRIPTURES

Use the space below each Power Scripture to translate them into your own personal confession of faith and the action you will take. Keep in mind that your faith can be strengthened and your situation changed by applying God's Word.

Psalm 27:1 "A Psalm of David. The LORD *is* my light and my salvation; whom shall I fear? the LORD *is* the strength of my life; of whom shall I be afraid?" New International Version

Psalm 121:2 "I will lift up mine eyes unto the hills, from whence cometh my help. My help *cometh* from the LORD, which made heaven and earth."

Jeremiah 29:11 "For I know the thoughts that I think toward you, saith the LORD, thoughts of peace, and not of evil, to give you an expected end."

Isaiah 26:3 "Thou wilt keep *him* in perfect peace, *whose* mind *is* stayed *on thee*: because he trusteth in thee."

Matthew 11:28-29 "Come unto me, all *ye* that labour and are heavy laden, and I will give you rest. Take my yoke upon you, and learn of me; for I am meek and lowly in heart: and ye shall find rest unto your souls."

Romans 8:28 "And we know that all things work together for good to them that love God, to them who are the called according to his purpose."

Isaiah 54:17 "No weapon that is formed against thee shall prosper; and every tongue *that* shall rise against thee in judgment thou shalt condemn. This *is* the heritage of the servants of the LORD, and their righteousness *is* of me, saith the LORD."

Psalm 27:2-3 "When the wicked, even mine enemies and my foes, came upon me to eat up my flesh, they stumbled and fell. Though an host should encamp against me, my heart shall not fear: though war should rise against me, in this will I be confident."

Psalm 46:1b-2 "God *is* our refuge and strength, a very present help in trouble. Therefore we will not fear, though the earth be removed, and though the mountains be carried into the midst of the sea; *Though* the waters thereof roar *and* be troubled, *though* the mountains shake with the swelling thereof. Selah."

1ˢᵗ Peter 5:7 "Cast all your anxiety on him because he cares for you." New International Version

1ˢᵗ John 4:4 "You, dear children, are from God and have over-come them, because the one who is in you is greater than the one who is in the world." New International Version

Galatians 5:1 "Stand fast therefore in the liberty wherewith Christ hath made us free, and be not entangled again with the yoke of bondage."

James 1:2-3 "Consider it pure joy, my brothers and sisters, whenever you face trials of many kinds, because you know that the testing of your faith produces perseverance." New International Version

Hebrews 4:16 "Let us therefore come boldly unto the throne of grace, that we may obtain mercy, and find grace to help in time of need."

Philippians 4:6-7 "Do not be anxious about anything, but in every situation, by prayer and petition, with thanksgiving, present your requests to God. And the peace of God, which transcends all understanding, will guard your hearts and your minds in Christ Jesus." New International Version

Jeremiah 33:3 "Call unto me, and I will answer thee, and shew thee great and mighty things, which thou knowest not."

Psalm 126:5 "They that sow in tears shall reap in joy."

Psalm 37:4 "Delight thyself also in the LORD; and he shall give thee the desires of thine heart."

Matthew 19:26 "And looking at them Jesus said to them, 'With people this is impossible, but with God all things are possible.'"
New American Standard

Philippians 4:13 "I can do all things through Christ which strengtheneth me."

Mark 11:24 "Therefore I say unto you, What things soever ye desire, when ye pray, believe that ye receive *them*, and ye shall have *them*."

Isaiah 44:22 "I have blotted out, as a thick cloud, thy transgressions, and, as a cloud, thy sins: return unto me; for I have redeemed thee."

Isaiah 55:10-11 "For as the rain cometh down, and the snow from heaven, and returneth not thither, but watereth the earth, and maketh it bring forth and bud, that it may give seed to the sower, and bread to the eater: So shall my word be that goeth forth out of my mouth: it shall not return unto me void, but it shall accomplish that which I please, and it shall prosper in the thing whereto I sent it."

Hebrews 13:8 "Jesus Christ the same yesterday, and today, and forever."

Proverbs 18:10 "The name of the LORD is a strong tower: the righteous runneth into it, and is safe."

Isaiah 65:24 "And it shall come to pass, that before they call, I will answer; and while they are yet speaking, I will hear."

Matthew 21:22 "And whatever you ask in prayer, you will receive, if you have faith." English Standard Version

Hebrews 4:16 "So let us come boldly to the throne of our gracious God. There we will receive his mercy, and we will find grace to help us when we need it most." New Living Translation

Isaiah 40:31 "But they that wait upon the LORD shall renew their strength; they shall mount up with wings as eagles; they shall run, and not be weary; *and* they shall walk, and not faint."

James 1:16-17 "Do not err, my beloved brethren. Every good gift and every perfect gift is from above, and cometh down from the Father of lights, with whom is no variableness, neither shadow of turning."

Matthew 7:7-8 "Ask, and it shall be given you; seek, and ye shall find; knock, and it shall be opened unto you: For every one that asketh, receiveth; and he that seeketh findeth; and to him that knocketh it shall be opened."

James 1:5 "Now if any of you lacks wisdom, he should ask God, who gives to everyone generously without a rebuke, and it will be given to him." International Standard Version

1ˢᵗ John 5:14-15 "And this is the confidence that we have in him, that, if we ask any thing according to his will, he heareth us: And if we know that he hears us, whatsoever we ask, we know that we have the petitions that we desired of him."

Deuteronomy 31:8 "Do not be afraid or discouraged, for the LORD will personally go ahead of you. He will be with you; he will neither fail you nor abandon you." New Living Translation

Psalm 23:4 "Yea, though I walk through the valley of the shadow of death, I will fear no evil: for thou *art* with me; thy rod and thy staff they comfort me."

James 1:12 "God blesses those who patiently endure testing and temptation. Afterward they will receive the crown of life that God has promised to those who love him." New Living Translation

Isaiah 54:10 "For the mountains shall depart, and the hills be removed; but my kindness shall not depart from thee, neither shall the covenant of my peace be removed, saith the LORD that hath mercy on thee."

Psalm 42:5 "Why are you in despair, my soul? Why are you disturbed within me? Hope in God, for once again I will praise him, since his presence saves me." International Standard Version

<hr>

2nd Corinthians 5:7 "For we walk by faith, not by sight."

<hr>

Isaiah 43:18-19 "Remember ye not the former things, neither consider the things of old. Behold, I will do a new thing; now it shall spring forth; shall ye not know it? I will even make a way in the wilderness, *and* rivers in the desert."

<hr>

Ephesians 6:10-17 "Finally, be strong in the Lord and in his mighty power. Put on the full armor of God, so that you can take your stand against the devil's schemes. For our struggle is not against flesh and blood, but against the rulers, against the authorities, against the powers of this dark world and against the spiritual forces of evil in the heavenly realms. Therefore put on the full armor of God, so that when the day of evil comes, you may be able to stand your ground, and after you have done everything, to stand. Stand firm then, with the belt of truth buckled around your waist, with the breastplate of righteousness in place, and with your feet fitted with the readiness that comes from the gospel of peace. In

addition to all this, take up the shield of faith, with which you can extinguish all the flaming arrows of the evil one. Take the helmet of salvation and the sword of the Spirit, which is the word of God." New International Version

Psalm 23 "The Lord is my shepherd, I lack nothing. He makes me lie down in green pastures, he leads me beside quiet waters, he refreshes my soul. He guides me along the right paths for his name's sake. Even though I walk through the darkest valley, I will fear no evil, for you are with me; your rod and your staff, they comfort me. You prepare a table before me in the presence of my enemies. You anoint my head with oil; my cup overflows. Surely your goodness and love will follow me all the days of my life, and I will dwell in the house of the Lord forever." New International Version

SPECIFIC POWER SCRIPTURES

Apply these Specific Power Scriptures to specific situations in your life. Personalize and confess them as a declaration of God's power and your faith. Be sure to include them in your prayers.

CLOSENESS TO GOD

Psalm 145:18-19 "The LORD *is* nigh unto all them that call upon him, to all that call upon him in truth. He will fulfil the desire of them that fear him: he also will hear their cry, and will save them."

ENCOURAGEMENT

Isaiah 41:13 "For I the LORD thy God will hold thy right hand, saying unto thee, Fear not; I will help thee."

OBSTACLES REMOVED

Isaiah 45:2 "I will go before you and make the rough places smooth; I will shatter the doors of bronze and cut through their iron bars." New American Standard Bible

Matthew 21:20-21 "Seeing this, the disciples were amazed and asked, 'How did the fig tree wither all at once?' And Jesus answered and said to them, 'Truly I say to you, if you have faith and do not doubt, you will not only do what was done to the fig tree, but even if you say to this mountain, 'Be taken up and cast into the sea,' it will happen.'" New American Standard Bible

STRENGTH IN WEAKNESS

Isaiah 41:10 "Fear thou not; for I *am* with thee: be not dismayed; for I *am* thy God: I will strengthen thee; yea, I will help thee; yea, I will uphold thee with the right hand of my righteousness."

PERSEVERANCE

2ⁿᵈ Timothy 2:1 "Thou therefore, my son, be strong in the grace that is in Christ Jesus."

Ephesians 6:10 "Finally, my brethren, be strong in the Lord, and in the power of his might."

JOY AND HAPPINESS

Psalm 16:11 "Thou wilt shew me the path of life: in thy presence *is* fullness of joy; at thy right hand *there are* pleasures for evermore."

Galatians 6:9 "Let us not lose heart in doing good, for in time we will reap if we do not grow weary." New American Standard Bible

GOD'S HELP

John 16:24 "Until now you have asked for nothing in My name; ask and you will receive, so that your joy may be made full." New American Standard Bible

John 14:14 "If ye shall ask any thing in my name, I will do *it*."

GOD'S CARE

Matthew 10:30-31 "But the very hairs of your head are all numbered. Fear ye not therefore, ye are of more value than many sparrows."

1st Peter 5:7 "Casting all your care upon him; for he careth for you."

GOD'S GRACE

2nd Corinthians 12:9a "Each time he said, 'My grace is all you need. My power works best in weakness.'" New Living Translation

WISDOM

James 1:5-6 "If any of you lacks wisdom, you should ask God, who gives generously to all without finding fault, and it will be given to you. But when you ask, you must believe and not doubt, because the one who doubts is like a wave of the sea, blown and tossed by the wind." New International Version

---

GOD'S PRESENCE

Genesis 28:15 "Now pay attention! I'm here with you, and I'm going to be watching over you wherever you go. I'm going to bring you back to this land, because I won't ever leave you until I've accomplished what I've promised about you." International Standard Version

---

TRUSTING GOD

Psalm 37:5 "Commit your way to the LORD; Trust him, and he will act." International Standard Version

Psalm 118:8 "*It is* better to trust in the LORD than to put confidence in man."

COURAGE DURING TRIALS

Isaiah 43:2 "When thou passest through the waters, I *will be* with thee; and through the rivers, they shall not overflow thee: when thou walkest through the fire, thou shalt not be burned; neither shall the flame kindle upon thee."

GOD'S FAITHFULNESS

1ˢᵗ Corinthians 1:9 "God *is* faithful, by whom ye were called unto the fellowship of his Son Jesus Christ our Lord."

Hebrews 10:23 "Let us hold fast the profession of *our* faith without wavering; (for he *is* faithful that promised)."

DIVINE GUIDANCE

Proverbs 3:5 "Trust in the LORD with all thine heart; and lean not unto thine own understanding. In all thy ways acknowledge him and he shall direct thy paths.

Proverbs 16:3 "Commit your actions to the LORD, and your plans will succeed."

GOD'S PROTECTION

Deuteronomy 3:22 "Ye shall not fear them: for the LORD your

God he shall fight for you."

HELP IN TROUBLING TIMES

Psalm 27:3 "Though a host encamp against me, My heart will not fear; Though war arise against me, In spite of this I shall be confident." New American Standard

---

Psalm 27:5 "For in the day of trouble He will conceal me in His tabernacle; In the secret place of His tent He will hide me; He will lift me up on a rock."

FEAR

Proverbs 3:25-26 "Be not afraid of sudden fear, neither of the desolation of the wicked, when it cometh. For the LORD shall be thy confidence, and shall keep thy foot from being taken."

DELIVERANCE

Psalm 60:4-5 "Thou hast given a banner to them that fear thee, that it may be displayed because of the truth. Selah. That thy beloved may be delivered; save *with* thy right hand, and hear me."

FAMILY BLESSING

Isaiah 44:3-4 "For I will pour water on the thirsty land, and streams on the dry ground; I will pour my Spirit upon your offspring, and my blessing on your descendants. They shall spring up among the grass like willows by flowing streams." English Standard Edition

Proverbs 11:21 "Though hand join in hand, the evil man shall not be unpunished; But the seed of the righteous shall be delivered." American Standard Version

HEALING

Jeremiah 17:14 "Heal me, O LORD, and I shall be healed; save me, and I shall be saved: for thou *art* my praise."

FORGIVENESS

1st John 1:9 "If we confess our sins, he is faithful and just to forgive us *our* sins, and to cleanse us from all unrighteousness."

NEED OF SALVATION

2nd Corinthians 6:2 "For He says: I heard you in an acceptable time, and I helped you in the day of salvation. Look, now is the acceptable time; now is the day of salvation." Holman Christian Standard Bible

Romans 10:9-10 "That if you confess with your mouth Jesus as Lord, and believe in your heart that God raised Him from the dead, you will be saved; for with the heart a person believes, resulting in righteousness, and with the mouth he confesses, resulting in salvation." New American Standard Bible

RESTORATION

Psalm 51:11-12 "Renew a loyal spirit within me. Do not banish me from your presence, and don't take your Holy Spirit from me. Restore to me the joy of your salvation, and make me willing to obey you." New Living Translation

DEDICATION AND RE-DEDICATION TO CHRIST

While in *"the Secret Place of the Most High,* make a decision to commit your life to Christ who is able to do more for you than you can ever ask or even think.

Ephesians 3:20 "Now unto him that is able to do exceeding abundantly above all that we ask or think, according to the power that worketh in us."

You've learned through this devotional study how to become closer to God so that you can be sure of His Divine help during your times of trouble. However, you will not realize and receive the fullness of this without accepting His gift of Salvation which is freely given through His only begotten Son … Jesus Christ.

John 3:16 "For God so loved the world, that he gave his only begotten Son, that whosoever believeth in him should not perish, but have everlasting life."

John 14:6 "Jesus saith unto him, I am the way, the truth, and the life: no man cometh unto the Father, but by me."

Now is the time to commit or recommit your life to Christ. Allow Him into your heart so that He takes control of your life, bringing you the security and fulfillment that God, your Heavenly Father, wants you to have.

Revelation 3:20 "Behold, I stand at the door, and knock: if any man hear my voice, and open the door, I will come in to him, and will sup with him, and he with me."

Romans 10:9-11 "That if thou shalt confess with thy mouth the Lord Jesus, and shalt believe in thine heart that God hath raised him from the dead, thou shalt be saved. For with the heart man believeth unto righteousness; and with the mouth confession is made unto salvation."

Say this prayer with an earnest and open heart:

"Father, I come to you now in the name of Jesus, who fulfilled your plan of redemption for me by dying on the cross for all of my sins. I accept Jesus and welcome Him into my heart as my Lord and Savior, allowing Him to take control of my life. I thank you Father, for saving me and giving me "new life." In Jesus' name, Amen."

I personally, give God thanks for your peace and victory.

God Bless You,
Dr. Walker

Visit www.yourspirituallife.org for spiritual life coaching, free downloads, inspirational Bible Studies and discussions.

Also Available in this Study Devotional Series to empower your spiritual life further:

WHEN YOU PRAY ... PRAY LIKE THIS
What, When, How ... All you need to know about prayer is in this study devotional

FROM GLORY TO GLORY ... CHANGE AND TRANSITION
A study devotional that explains change and transition to help you fulfill your destiny

To Learn More about the Bible order:

THE INTRODUCTION SERIES:

Introduction to Bible Doctrine
A Systematic Study of Seven Doctrines of the Christian Faith – Made Easy

Introduction to Bible Origin
A Study of the Formation of the Bible

Introduction to Typology and Symbolism
An Expository Study of Types and Symbols Found in the Bible

To Receive a Certificate in Biblical Studies:
   Go to: *www.theinstituteoftheology.org*

www.ingramcontent.com/pod-product-compliance
Lightning Source LLC
Chambersburg PA
CBHW071842020426
42331CB00007B/1822